DUE DATE

DISCARD

PARTHENON

PARTHENON

LYNN CURLEE

ATHENEUM BOOKS FOR YOUNG READERS

NEW YORK LONDON TORONTO SYDNEY

It is one of the greatest sights in the world—the lofty, barren, windswept rock encircled by massive ramparts, the flat terraces of its summit encrusted with the weathered stones of ancient shrines. On its highest crest, the rock is crowned with the stained and battered ruins of a magnificent marble temple, a vivid landmark that dominates the surrounding city and countryside. The people of ancient Greece called the rocky citadel the Acropolis, the "High City." It was their fortress, their stronghold, their civic center, and their most holy sanctuary, sacred to Athena, goddess of wisdom, who gave her name to the city of Athens below. The temple was built as an offering to her—Athena Parthenos, warrior-maiden, guardian of her city. It came to be called the Parthenon.

Ancient Athens was the center of one of the most brilliant explosions of creativity in human history. Our grand tradition of western literature began with two great epic poems, the *Iliad* and the *Odyssëy*, first written down by the legendary Greek poet Homer. Authors such as Herodotus and Thucydides were among the first to record historical facts accurately. The art of theater was first practiced in Athens. Tragic dramas by Sophocles, Aeschylus, and Euripides are still performed today. Socrates, Plato, and Aristotle, great philosophers of the time, conceived new ways of asking questions and solving intellectual problems. The mathematician Pythagoras tried to demonstrate that all things can be expressed by numbers. Scientific inquiry first began with close observation of the natural world by Greek thinkers. In the realm of politics the idea of democracy was conceived by the ancient Athenians. And all of these accomplishments have been passed down through the ages to our modern world. The achievements of the ancient Greeks in art, architecture, literature, drama, history, philosophy, science, and politics were so profound that today the Acropolis of Athens is considered to be the birthplace of western civilization.

The Acropolis of Athens today.

The Parthenon is the supreme architectural and artistic masterpiece of the golden age of ancient Greece. It has long been considered by many to be the most beautiful and important building in the world and has been called the most perfect structure ever erected. It was also adorned with some of the greatest sculpture ever carved. Miraculously, enough of it has survived through the centuries that today we can still glimpse a trace of its original splendor. The Acropolis of Athens with its glorious ruins is one of the magical places of mankind.

In Greek mythology there is a story of a contest between the goddess Athena and the god Poseidon, lord of the sea. Whoever gave the greater gift to mankind would win the Acropolis. Poseidon struck the summit of the rocky citadel with his trident, and a spring began to flow. Athena then caused the first olive tree to grow beside the spring. An assembly of gods decreed that Athena's was the greater gift, and the Acropolis became hers.

People have lived on or around the sacred rock since the beginning of recorded history. Thirty-five centuries ago, Bronze Age warrior-kings fortified the hill with battlements and built their palaces on the summit. Nearly a millennium later, the rulers of Athens adorned the Acropolis with shrines and temples. At first these were simple brick-and-timber structures, but gradually they were replaced by buildings made of stone.

By 500 B.C. Athens was a proud and prosperous city-state governed by an assembly of the people. Although limited to male citizens (women, slaves, and non-Greeks were not considered citizens), it was the first democracy in the world. By now the entire Acropolis was given over to the worship of the gods. It was the center of Athens's religious life as well as the focus of civic pride. In addition, its sheer walls guarded the wealth of the city, which was held in the store-houses of the various temples.

The mythical contest between Athena and Poseidon.

In the early fifth century B.C. Greece was invaded by the armies of the Persian Empire. The Persian Wars lasted for forty years, and in the first campaign, at the Battle of Marathon, the Persian battalions were soundly defeated by a small force of Athenians. In the moment of triumph, they decided to build a new stone temple in honor of Athena on the summit of the Acropolis. Marble for this temple was quarried, foundations were laid, and construction began. Archaeologists call it the Pre-Parthenon because ten years after Marathon, in 480 B.C., the Persians returned. Their target was Athens. Construction on the Pre-Parthenon ceased, and it was never finished.

The Athenians realized that this time the Persians would win a battle on land, so the people fled, abandoning their city to the enemy. The Athenian navy then lured the Persian fleet into a great sea battle at the Bay of Salamis near Athens. The big lumbering Persian ships were no match for the Athenian vessels, which were small, light, and built to ram and sink the enemy. The Persian emperor Xerxes watched from a hill overlooking the bay as his navy was crushed. The Greeks were victorious again, but they paid a terrible price. Athens had been sacked, the Acropolis and its temples looted and burned. The Greeks took a solemn oath to leave the temples in ruins as a memorial to the dead and as a reminder of the sacrilege of the Persians.

This oath was binding for thirty years while the conflict with Persia continued in other parts of the Greek world. Athens became the leader of the Delian League, an association of city-states united against the Persian threat. As the most powerful city with the largest navy, Athens protected the other cities of the League in return for tribute, a kind of tax. Over time, the surplus tribute money filled the coffers of the Athenian treasury. When peace finally was established with Persia in 449 B.C., Athens was very wealthy and took control of the League. The Delian League had become the Athenian Empire.

Also at this time an aristocrat named Pericles was the leader of the democratic assembly of Athens. He was determined to have the city take back its oath and rebuild the Acropolis using the

The Greeks defeat the Persians at the Bay of Salamis.

surplus tribute money. He argued that the greatest city in Greece deserved magnificent buildings as a symbol of her power. Although he encountered fierce opposition from those who felt that such a lavish display would be immodest, Pericles was a good politician and a great statesman, and he managed to push his grand plan through the assembly. The entire Acropolis was to be reconstructed, with the addition of a new monumental gateway guarding the single entrance leading into the citadel, and, most importantly, a grand new temple to Athena crowning the summit.

A project of this scale was a vast undertaking involving every member of society. Besides adorning the city, Pericles intended the rebuilding of the Acropolis to be a huge public works project in which every person would benefit. The Greek historian Plutarch tells us of the artists and trades-men who were involved. "There were smiths and carpenters, moulders, founders and braziers, stonecutters, dyers, goldsmiths, ivory-workers, painters, embroiderers, turners; and those that con-veyed them to the town for use, merchants and mariners and shipmasters by sea, and by land, cartwrights, cattle-breeders, waggoners, rope-makers, flax-workers, shoemakers and leather-dressers, road-makers, and miners. And every trade had its own hired company of journeymen and laborers." Interestingly, records tell us that the men who worked on the Acropolis were all paid the same wage, whether architects or common laborers, citizens or slaves.

Work began immediately on the great temple. Athens's leading artist was a great sculptor named Phidias. About ten years before the Acropolis's reconstruction, he had fashioned a monumental bronze statue of Athena. A magnificent armed figure thirty feet tall, she was set up outside on the Acropolis as a memorial to the victories over the Persians. It is said that the tip of her spear glint-ing in the sunlight could be seen from ships at sea ten miles away. Until now, this statue had been Phidias's greatest accomplishment. Then he was put in charge of the entire Acropolis project.

Phidias's bronze statue of Athena on the Acropolis.

With Phidias named overseer of the project, two men were then appointed architects of the Parthenon—Ictinus and Callicrates. Ictinus probably was the main designer, and Callicrates the master builder. Pericles, Phidias, Ictinus, and Callicrates certainly worked very closely together. The first decision they made was to use the existing foundations and the remaining undamaged blocks of marble already quarried for the Pre-Parthenon. This enabled them to start building quickly and save an enormous amount of money. The marble quarries were ten miles from Athens on Mount Pentelicus, and transporting massive stone blocks, each weighing many tons, was one of the most expensive parts of building a Greek temple. The new building was to be somewhat larger than the Pre-Parthenon, so the foundations were extended, and as the Parthenon was constructed, an additional 20,000 tons of marble were quarried and transported by oxcart to the Acropolis.

All Greek temples are very similar in design. They all have basically the same parts and every part has a proper name. There is a central rectangular chamber (the *cella*) with solid walls and a front porch (the *pronaos*). Large temples might also have a rear porch. The cella is surrounded by a continuous row of columns (the *peristyle*) that supports the upper parts of the building (the *entablature*) on massive horizontal beams (the *architrave*). A low-pitched tile roof covers the entire building, and at each end, there is a gable (the *pediment*). A Greek temple is essentially a very simple type of structure, but as soon as Greek architects began building with stone instead of with brick and timber in about 600 B.C., they developed standard complex shapes for the columns, the entablature, and all of the other various parts of their temples. Some scholars believe that these patterns and shapes carved in stone were meant to copy the wooden structure of the older temples.

These sophisticated systems of design are called the Orders of Architecture, and they rapidly became quite fixed. Working within these rigid orders, an architect made his building unique by experimenting with the proportions and adjusting the scale of the various parts. At first there were

THE PARTHENON

CROSS SECTION

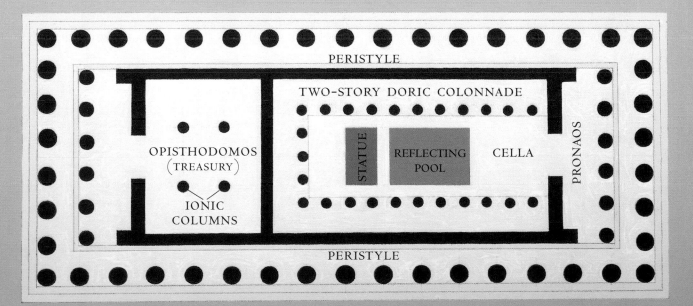

PERISTYLE

TWO-STORY DORIC COLONNADE

OPISTHODOMOS
(TREASURY)

STATUE

REFLECTING
POOL

CELLA

PRONAOS

IONIC
COLUMNS

PERISTYLE

FOOTPRINT

only two orders—the Doric and the Ionic. The Doric Order was considered a more masculine style. It was massive, formal, and severe. The Ionic Order was considered more feminine. It was lighter, prettier, and more decorative. All Greek temples were built using one of the orders.

The Parthenon was the largest and most elaborate of all Doric temples. Except for the wooden roof beams and the interior ceilings, it was built entirely of marble. Even the roof tiles were marble, a rare extravagance. The Parthenon had eight columns on each end, and seventeen along each side. Most other large Doric temples had only six columns on each end and thirteen on the sides. It had a wide cella and an unusual feature—a smaller rear chamber (the *opisthodomos*).

A Greek temple was not a church. It was built as an offering to a specific god or goddess, and housed and protected the sacred statue of the deity to whom it was dedicated. Ceremonies and sacrifices were held outdoors at great altars, and the temple was a backdrop for the ritual. The interior chambers of the Parthenon, with their solid walls, were dark and enclosed, accessible only through great bronze doors. The opisthodomos served as a treasury, a storehouse for the city's riches. Four slender Ionic columns held up the ceiling. Using the Ionic Order inside a Doric temple was a new and radical idea to Greek architects. The main cella was designed to hold a great statue of Athena, to be made by Phidias himself. Its wooden ceiling was supported by a two-story colonnade of Doric columns, which framed the enormous figure.

Ictinus and Callicrates probably did not work from elaborate drawings like architects do today. There may have been some preliminary drawings to calculate the proportions, but the layout probably was done directly on the foundations. To convey their ideas to the stonemasons, the architects constructed a *paradigm*, most likely a set of full-scale stone models of the exact details of the building for the stonecarvers to copy.

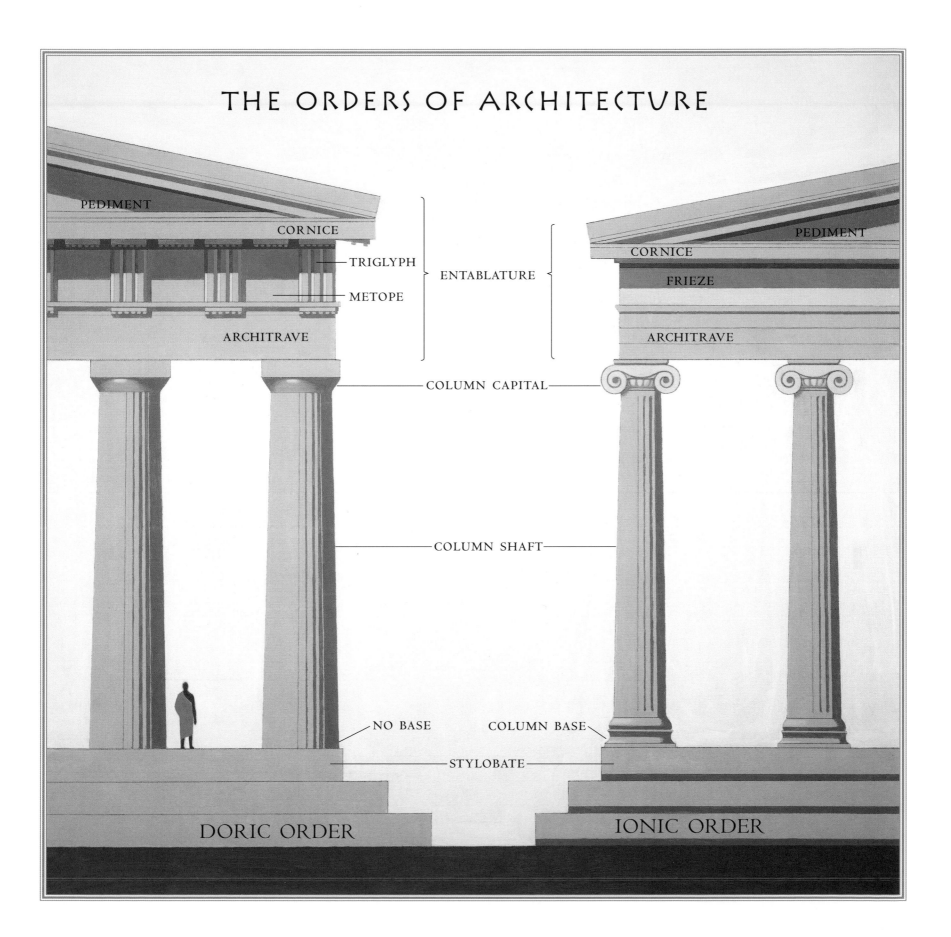

THE ORDERS OF ARCHITECTURE

PEDIMENT

CORNICE

TRIGLYPH

METOPE

ENTABLATURE

ARCHITRAVE

CORNICE

PEDIMENT

FRIEZE

ARCHITRAVE

COLUMN CAPITAL

COLUMN SHAFT

NO BASE

COLUMN BASE

STYLOBATE

DORIC ORDER

IONIC ORDER

The construction of the Parthenon began with the peristyle. The accurate spacing of the columns was of critical importance for the proportions of the upper parts of the building. Greek architects used no mortar to construct their temples. They carved the stones with extreme precision and rested one layer upon another as the building rose. Metal clamps were used here and there between stones to prevent shifting. A Greek temple is held in place only by gravity. Huge marble building blocks weighing many tons were moved about and hoisted using the most basic equipment—rollers, sledges, levers, wedges, ropes, pulleys, and simple winches. Marble can be carved with great finesse, and every detail was exact and precise, the joints between blocks nearly invisible. The stonework of the Parthenon was of the very highest quality.

A Doric temple, with its regular array of columns and massive entablature, can appear somewhat static and heavy, but the Parthenon, even in ruins, seems buoyant and alive. This is because Ictinus and Callicrates built into the structure certain details called *refinements*. Amazingly there are almost no straight lines in the Parthenon. All four sides of the platform (the *stylobate*) on which the temple was built have a slight but visible upward curve in the center. This subtle curve is carried up through the different parts of the building. No horizontal lines are absolutely straight. The columns themselves do not have straight sides either. They swell outward very slightly as if straining under the weight of the heavy entablature. In addition the corner columns are closer to their neighbors, and are also somewhat thicker than the others. Every column leans inward very slightly. It has been determined that if the corner columns continued upward into the air, they would meet one and one half miles above the earth.

Unless they are pointed out, the refinements are almost invisible, but all of these fine details affect how the Parthenon "feels" to us. Besides requiring incredibly intricate calculations, constructing the refinements meant that every stone had to be carved slightly irregularly but with exquisite

THE REFINEMENTS
(SHOWN GREATLY EXAGGERATED)

ALL HORIZONTAL LINES
CURVE UPWARD IN THE CENTER

COLUMNS SWELL SLIGHTLY
AND LEAN INWARD

CORNER COLUMNS
ARE SLIGHTLY THICKER
AND ARE CLOSER
TO THEIR NEIGHBORS

precision to fit its specific spot. This made the Parthenon much more expensive than it would have been otherwise. The care lavished on the workmanship and the refinements built into its design transformed this basically simple structure into one of the most complex, subtle, and sophisticated buildings ever constructed.

The glory of the Parthenon was its sculptural decoration. The upper parts of the building were practically encrusted with carved figures. Like most Doric temples, the Parthenon had a grouping of large statues in each pediment, but every one of its 92 *metopes* was carved as well. Metopes are flat panels that alternate with grooved panels called *triglyphs* in every Doric entablature. Most remarkable of all, there was an Ionic style *frieze*, a continuous band around the outside top of the cella walls, completely and lavishly filled with relief sculpture. No other Doric temple had anything like it. Finally there were roof sculptures (the *acroteria*)—a figure standing on each corner of the roof with a huge crest on the peak at each end. As on all Greek temples, the sculptures and certain details of the architecture were brightly painted and gilded.

As overseer of the entire Acropolis project, Phidias may have been the master designer for all of the sculptures, but they were actually carved by teams of sculptors recruited from all over the Greek world. By the time the Parthenon's construction began in 447 B.C., the Acropolis workshops must have been full of artists and their assistants, already hard at work carving the 92 metopes. About four feet square, each metope had to be finished and in place before the roof could go on. Most of the panels showed two figures fighting: gods fighting giants; Greeks fighting Trojans; Athenians fighting warrior-women called Amazons; and men fighting monstrous centaurs who were half man, half horse. The figures were shown in violent action, and were sculpted in extremely high relief. On the building they stood out sharply from their backgrounds, which were painted red. The alternating

A detail of a corner of the Parthenon, showing a winged Victory acroterium.

triglyphs were painted blue. These sculptures of famous mythological battles symbolized the victory of the civilized Greeks over the barbaric Persians.

The Parthenon's frieze is considered by many to be her crowning glory. At nearly 525 feet long and a little over 3 feet high, it has 1,700 square feet of carving. It shows the people of Athens participating in a great procession during the Panathenea, a religious festival of athletic games, theatrical events, and musical concerts that was celebrated every four years. The festival culminated in the Panathenaic procession, a grand parade to the Acropolis where a new garment called a *peplos*, woven by selected Athenian maidens, was dedicated to Athena. On the Parthenon's frieze, originally against a painted blue background, the carved scene of more than 400 men and women and 200 animals begins with a grand cavalcade of riders on glorious, spirited horses. It continues with wheeling chariots and marching musicians. Athenian youths bear pitchers and trays of offerings, and lead sacrificial animals. Groups of elders and maidens move in a stately rhythm. The parade ends over the main entrance of the cella with the peplos ceremony attended by the great gods and goddesses of Mount Olympus, seated upon their thrones. The frieze is one of the greatest masterpieces of sculpture ever carved, but ironically, since the figures were placed high up under the shade of the peristyle, they must have been difficult to see from the ground below.

The most imposing sculptures on the Parthenon were the magnificent groups of statues, twice lifesize, that filled the triangular spaces of the east and west pediments. There were more than twenty statues in each one. The east pediment showed the birth of Athena. According to myth, she sprang fully grown from the head of Zeus, king of the gods. On the pediment, this strange event was shown having just taken place. Athena stood beside Zeus, surrounded by other gods and goddesses. The west pediment held the fabled contest between Athena and Poseidon for the Acropolis. They confronted each other in the center of the pediment, while various deities and the ancient kings of Athens looked on.

A sculptor at work on a portion of the frieze.

The exterior of the Parthenon was finished off with intricately carved floral crests about nine feet tall, which were set upon the peak of each pediment. Archaeologists have found pieces of them. It was long believed that a smaller crest stood on each corner of the roof, but scholars now think that these corner acroteria were winged Victory figures poised in flight.

Although horribly battered, many metopes have survived over the centuries, and large portions of the frieze exist in fair condition. But the pediment statues have suffered the most damage. The important central statues have largely disappeared. What remains are only a few mutilated figures and many fragments, but these are still astonishing and incredibly beautiful. Even broken into pieces, these sculptures are full of life and movement. They were carved with deep feeling and a spirit of lofty nobility. Even their backs were fully carved, although once in place high up on the temple's pediment, they would never be seen.

In 438 B.C., only nine years after construction began on the Parthenon, Phidias's colossal new statue was completed and dedicated to Athena. An enormous figure nearly forty feet high, she was even larger than the great sculptor's earlier bronze Athena, which stood outside on the Acropolis nearby. This new statue of the goddess was placed on a pedestal in the center of the cella, her shield and spear at her left side. She wore a long peplos garment with her *aegis*, a kind of breastplate, covering her chest. On her head was a magnificent triple-crested helmet, and her right hand held the figure of a winged Victory. At her feet a coiled python, symbol of the early kings of Athens, reared its head. The statue's pedestal was decorated with figures from the famous myth of the birth of Pandora, the first woman.

The outside of Athena's round shield was carved with the battle between the Athenians and the Amazons, and the inside surface was painted with the battle between gods and giants. Even the edges of the soles of the goddess's sandals were decorated with figures of men fighting centaurs.

Previous pages: A segment of the Parthenon frieze.   *A battered sculpture from the east pediment.*

In the center of Athena's aegis was the image of the severed head of Medusa, a monstrous, snake-haired Gorgon whose glance turned men to stone.

This incredible statue was the heart of the Parthenon, and Athens's greatest treasure. It was not sculpted of marble or cast in bronze like other statues, but was made of rare precious materials. The skin of the goddess was fashioned of exotic elephant ivory imported from Africa. Small panels were joined together and then carved. Her garments were made of thin plates of solid gold, beaten and molded into shape. Her eyes and other details were inlaid with jewels and precious stones. The statue was as expensive to make as the Parthenon itself. More than a ton of gold was used, and it could be removed for safekeeping because the plates of ivory and gold were only the outer surface of the statue. They were probably attached to a base of wooden panels that was carved into the shape of the figure. The structure itself was hollow, its individual parts held together by a scaffolding of timbers. The entire elaborate construction was supported by a massive pole like the mast of a ship that was set into a floor socket. In front of the sacred image, Phidias cleverly designed a large shallow reflecting pool. The water prevented the wood and ivory from drying out and cracking.

Since both ivory and gold can be crafted with extremely fine precision, we can be certain that every detail of the great statue was perfectly finished, every hair crisply carved, even her eyelashes. In the dim and mysterious interior of the cella, her magnificent, noble figure reflected in the sacred pool, Phidias's Athena must have been an almost unbelievable, awe-inspiring sight. The spectacular, glittering display of gold and jewels must have been simply staggering, and with her milky-white, almost translucent ivory flesh, and her blue-gray eyes made of sparkling gems, it must have seemed as though the goddess herself had stepped down from Mount Olympus.

After this splendid masterpiece, Phidias would later go on to fashion another huge ivory-and-gold

Assembling the statue of Athena inside the Parthenon.

statue, an enormous figure of Zeus, which was made for the god's temple at Olympia, where the original Olympic Games were held every four years in his honor. Phidias's Zeus was later considered one of the Seven Wonders of the Ancient World.

Work continued on the Parthenon for six more years after the dedication of Phidias's statue. The pediment sculptures and the acroteria were finished and installed. The entire building was dressed down to its final surface. The painting and gilding were done and finally in 432 B.C. every detail was complete. High above the city on the Acropolis, with its colorful sculpture and its perfect white marble columns gleaming against a bright blue sky, the newly completed Parthenon must have been a dazzling sight. It had taken only fifteen years to build everything, an amazingly short time for such an elaborate and complex structure. As Plutarch wrote: "The works grew up, stately in size and exquisite in form, the workmen striving to perfect the material and the design with the beauty of their workmanship; yet the most wonderful thing of all was the speed."

It would take another quarter century to finish the entire Acropolis. Construction on the Propylaea, the monumental Doric entrance gate to the citadel, was started before the Parthenon was finished. It was almost as magnificent as the Parthenon itself. After the gate's completion, a tiny temple to Athena Nike (Athena the Victor) was erected on the bastion beside the Propylaea. Too small for a peristyle, it had only a cella with a front and rear porch styled in the Ionic Order. The last structure to be built on Pericles's Acropolis was the Erechtheum. Constructed over several different sacred sites, including the spring of Poseidon and the olive tree of Athena, it was a very unusual Ionic temple with a different entrance for each of its various shrines. One of these was the famous Porch of the Maidens. Instead of columns, statues called *caryatids* bore the entablature on their heads. These stately young women, perhaps representing the weavers of Athena's sacred peplos, looked directly across the Acropolis

Previous pages: The great ivory-and-gold statue of Athena by Phidias.　　　　　　　　*The newly completed Parthenon.*

to the Parthenon. When the Erechtheum was finished in 405 B.C., Pericles's glorious Acropolis was complete, but by then both he and Phidias were no longer living, and Athens was again at war, this time with her Greek rival, the city-state of Sparta. The great city's golden age was over.

During the rest of antiquity the Acropolis and its magnificent temple were honored, admired, and maintained. A century after the Parthenon was built, Alexander the Great gave to Athens a set of bronze shields that were mounted on the temple's architrave. A few centuries after that the Roman emperor Nero had an inscription honoring himself attached between the shields in letters made of bronze. The inscription was removed as soon as Nero was dead, but the holes for these attachments can still be seen on the building.

Then, sometime in the third century A.D. disaster struck. There is no written record of it, but archaeologists have determined that the wooden rafters of the Parthenon caught fire, and the heavy marble roof caved in. It is probable that Phidias's great statue of Athena was utterly destroyed in this catastrophe. Its golden peplos and jewels had certainly been stripped away for their value and replaced with copper and colored glass long before the fire. The temple remained in a ruined condition for about a century. When extensive repairs finally were made, a new roof was constructed, but only over the cella and the treasury. The peristyle was left roofless. Soon afterward, in A.D. 397, the Christian Roman emperor Theodosius I banned the worship of the ancient gods and goddesses. After 835 years as a temple to the goddess Athena, the doors of the Parthenon were closed.

The ancient world ended with the fall of Rome and the rise of Christianity. During the sixth century A.D. Athena's Parthenon was turned into a Christian church dedicated to the Virgin Mary, Our Lady of Athens. The early Christians didn't value the ancient sculptures. They defaced and mutilated many of the metopes, and in expanding the cella for their altar, they destroyed the central portion of the eastern

MAP OF THE ACROPOLIS

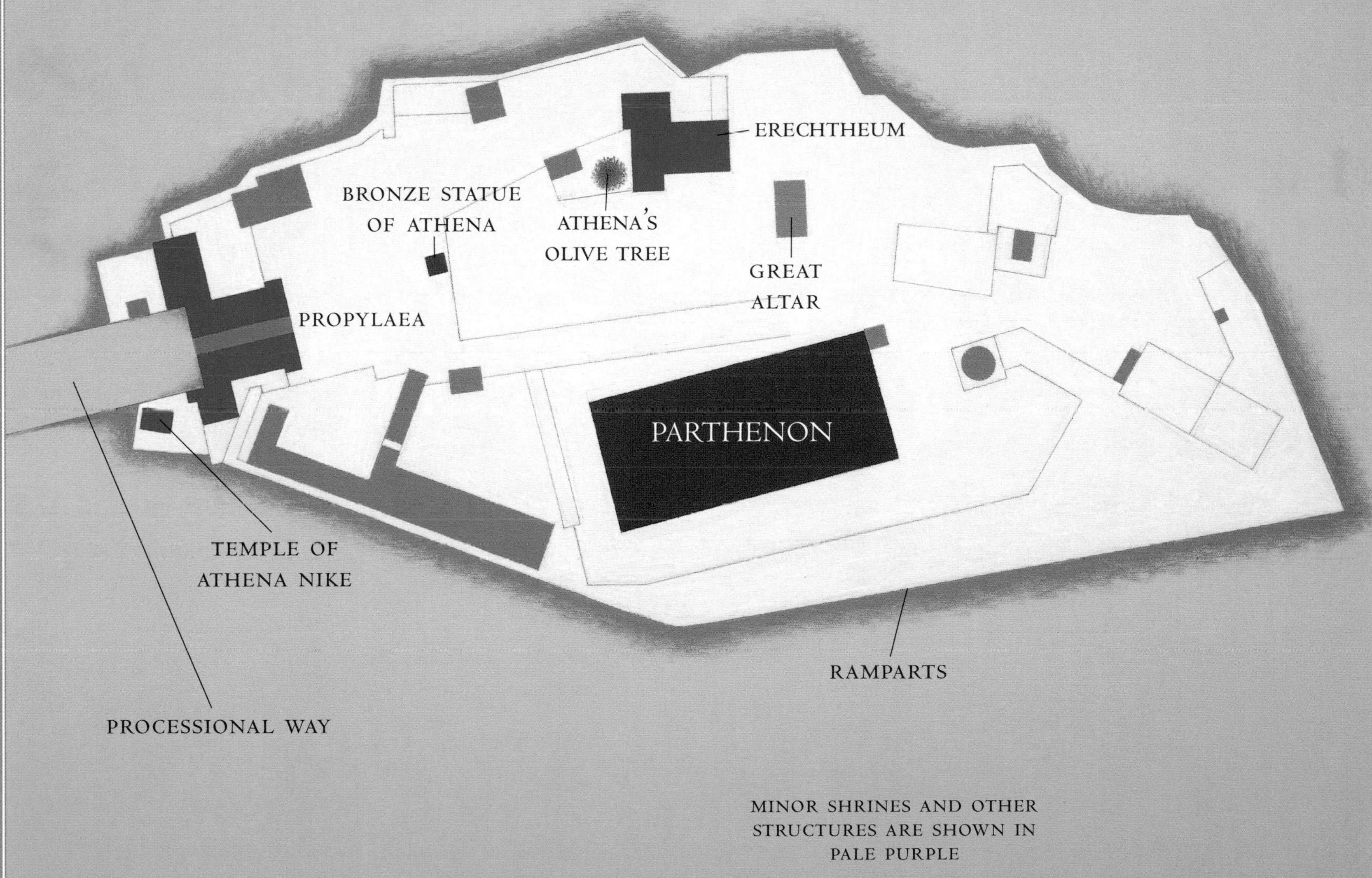

ERECHTHEUM

BRONZE STATUE
OF ATHENA

ATHENA'S
OLIVE TREE

GREAT
ALTAR

PROPYLAEA

PARTHENON

TEMPLE OF
ATHENA NIKE

RAMPARTS

PROCESSIONAL WAY

MINOR SHRINES AND OTHER
STRUCTURES ARE SHOWN IN
PALE PURPLE

pediment, with its great scene of the birth of Athena. But by converting the temple into a church, they also saved it. As long as it was being used, the Parthenon would not be completely destroyed.

By the Middle Ages in Europe, Athens was a backwater, her glorious past nearly forgotten. Over the centuries, control of the city and its Acropolis passed from the Byzantine emperors to the Frankish crusaders to the Spanish court to the dukes of Florence. In 1458 Athens was conquered yet again, this time by the Turkish Ottoman Empire. The Parthenon was transformed once more, into an Islamic mosque. A slender *minaret*, a tower for calling the faithful to prayer, was erected within the peristyle.

The Ottoman Turks controlled Athens for nearly 400 years, but they were not years of peace. On September 26, 1687, during a war between the Turks and the army of the city of Venice, a mortar shell pierced the roof of the Parthenon, igniting supplies of gunpowder that were stored there. A tremendous explosion destroyed the center of the great temple. The cella walls were shattered, 28 columns were toppled, massive architrave beams crashed to the pavement, and the roof was blown away. Large segments of the frieze and many metopes were lost. And it was all for nothing. The Venetians ruled for only one year before the Turks regained control of the city. After two millennia in almost constant use, the Parthenon was now only a battered ruin.

Sometime in the early 1700s, a small new mosque with tiled domes was constructed in the center of the Parthenon's ruins. By this time the entire Acropolis was covered with small houses and buildings, constructed during the passing centuries among the fallen blocks of stone and within the broken walls of the ancient shrines.

The eighteenth century in western Europe is known today as the Age of Enlightenment. There was renewed interest in the ancient Greek world. Scholars began to study the history, architects began to study the monuments, tourists began to visit Athens, and by the end of the century, collectors

The explosion of 1687.

were poking about among the ruins of famous sites and removing many interesting and beautiful objects. It was the beginning of the science of archaeology.

In 1801 Lord Elgin, British Ambassador to Constantinople, convinced the Turks to grant him a special permit "to take away from the Acropolis any pieces of stone with old inscriptions or figures thereon." Elgin proceeded to strip most of the remaining sculptures from the sad ruins of the Parthenon. He took numerous metopes, large segments of the frieze, and almost all of the few remaining pediment statues and fragments. He also took one of the beautiful caryatids from the Erechtheum.

The hoard of sculpture arrived in England in 1812. Lord Elgin had wanted to decorate his country estate with it, but when he needed money he sold his booty to the British Museum. When they were put on display in 1816, the sculptures, called the Elgin Marbles, were an instant sensation. The ancient Greek style became very fashionable, but more importantly, these battered and mutilated treasures from the Parthenon were finally recognized as part of one of the greatest achievements of mankind. They also became the center of a bitter controversy. Lord Byron, the famous poet, led the assault by accusing Elgin of robbing Greece of its precious national heritage. While it is true that Lord Elgin took what was not his, it is equally true that if he had not, the great sculptures would have been taken by someone else, or if left on the building, they would have deteriorated badly. By taking them, Elgin inadvertently preserved them. These sculptures are the greatest treasure of the British Museum, but many people still feel that the Elgin Marbles belong back in Greece. It is a controversy that still rages on to this day.

The Greek War of Independence from the Turks marks the beginning of the latest phase in the story of the Parthenon. In 1834 Athens became the capital of a liberated Greece, and the Acropolis was given over to archaeologists. During the next decades the medieval buildings and the houses

The Elgin Marbles in the British Museum.

and mosques of the Turks were removed. Everything added after antiquity was taken away, leaving only the bare rock and the classical ruins. Major scientific excavations began in about 1885. Eleven years later, in 1896, the Olympic Games were revived in Athens, and the attention of the world was focused on the Acropolis and its priceless heritage. The little temple of Athena Nike was reconstructed on its bastion, and work began on the remains of the Erechtheum and the Propylaea. Gradually, in a series of different campaigns, the ruins of the Parthenon were restored. Cella walls were rebuilt, column drums restacked, and architrave beams hoisted high into the air to span the columns. Except for those major parts that were blown away or shattered by explosion and fire, and with virtually all of its decoration stripped away, the skeletal remains of the world's greatest building have been carefully reassembled.

During the twentieth century the marble suffered great damage from the polluted air of modern Athens, and today the Parthenon is vigilantly monitored. The restoration and maintenance of its ruins continues with new archaeological discoveries and modern techniques. The Acropolis, the holy sanctuary of ancient Athens and birthplace of western civilization, has now become an inspiring outdoor museum for tourists. The Parthenon is the focus of Greek national pride, but truly it belongs to all of mankind. When construction of the Parthenon began twenty-five centuries ago, Pericles pledged to his fellow citizens, "We shall be the marvel of the present day and of ages yet to come." His proud boast has come true. Athena's magnificent temple remains one of the most triumphant achievements of the human spirit. Written five hundred years after Greece's golden age, Plutarch's words say it best: "It was created in a short time for all time. It was at once antique in its beauty, but in its vigour fresh and newly cut even today. Such is the bloom of youth upon it that it looks always untouched by time, as if it were suffused with unfailing life, and a spirit that cannot grow old."

The ruins of the Parthenon.

BIBLIOGRAPHY

Ashmole, Bernard. *Architect and Sculptor in Classical Greece.* New York: New York University Press, 1972.

Boardman, John. *Greek Sculpture: The Classical Period: A Handbook.* London: Thames and Hudson, 1985.

Coulton, J. J. *Ancient Greek Architects at Work: Problems of Structure and Design.* Ithaca, N.Y.: Cornell University Press, 1977.

Green, Peter, et. al., eds. *The Parthenon.* New York: Newsweek, 1973.

Stevens, G. P. *Restorations of Classical Buildings.* Princeton, N.J.: American School of Classical Studies at Athens, 1958.

Tournikiotis, Panayotis, ed. *The Parthenon and Its Impact in Modern Times.* Athens: Melissa, 1994.

Atheneum Books for Young Readers
An imprint of Simon & Schuster Children's Publishing Division
1230 Avenue of the Americas, New York, New York 10020
Copyright © 2004 by Lynn Curlee
All rights reserved, including the right of reproduction in whole or in part in any form.
Book design by Abelardo Martínez
The text of this book is set in Deepdene.
The illustrations are rendered in acrylic on canvas.
Mr. Curlee would like to thank Ed Peterson for photographing the paintings.
Manufactured in China
First Edition
2 4 6 8 10 9 7 5 3 1
Library of Congress Cataloging-in-Publication Data
Curlee, Lynn.
Parthenon / Lynn Curlee.—1st ed.
p. cm.
Summary: A detailed history of the Parthenon, exploring its construction and restoration.
ISBN 0-689-84490-5
1. Parthenon (Athens, Greece)—Juvenile literature. 2. Athens (Greece)—Buildings, structures, etc.—
Juvenile literature. [1. Parthenon (Athens, Greece) 2. Athens (Greece)—Antiquities.] I. Title.
NA281.C87 2004
726'.1208'09385—dc21
2003002615

Cover: The Parthenon today. Title spread: The Acropolis of Athens in ancient times.